Music Matters

AFRO-AMERICAN MUSIC

Clive D. Griffin

Dryad Press Limited   London

Typeset by Tek-Art Ltd, Kent
and printed by
R J Acford
Chichester, Sussex,
for the Publishers,
Dryad Press Limited,
8 Cavendish Square,
London W1M 0AJ

ISBN 0 8521 9701 2

ACKNOWLEDGMENTS

The Author and Publishers thank the following
for their kind permission to reproduce
copyright photographs: Edwin Baker, page 1;
The Bettmann Archive, BBC Hulton Picture
Library, pages 5, 24, 25, 26, 28, 29, 32, 37, 39,
41, 42, 43; BBC Hulton Picture Library
(Evening Standard Collection), page 31; The
Photo Source, pages 12, 14, 15, 30, 46, 49, 50,
51, 52, 59; The Royal Anthropological Institute
of Great Britain and Ireland, pages 7, 8;
Stern's, pages 57, 58. Many thanks also to
Melody Maker for help with the illustrations.
The maps on pages 10, 11, 22-23, 45, 48 and
56 were drawn by R.F. Brien.

The cover photograph of Aretha Franklin and
George Benson is reproduced courtesy of
Arista Records.

LUTON SIXTH FORM COLLEGE

-5. MAR. 1993	1 3 MAR 2003	
-2 NOV 1993	2 3 SEP 2003	
2 2 MAY 1996	1 6 SEP 2010	
10. SEP. 1996		
	- 4 SEP 2015	
-9. OCT. 1996		
-3 FEB. 1997		
16. OCT. 1998		
-9 NOV. 2000		
1 6 APR 2002		
1 0 MAY 2002		

This book is due for return on or before the last date shown above.

3-DAY ISSUE

3123

CONTENTS

INTRODUCTION

In the three hundred years between 1500 and 1800, millions of Africans were transported across the Atlantic to the European colonies in the Americas. The Africans carried their own culture and traditions with them but they also absorbed and adapted European ways. They blended their music with that of their oppressors to produce something different. Blues, gospel, soul, jazz, calypso, reggae – all grew from this mixture of African and European music. In some the European element is stronger, in others the African, but they are all forms of what we call AFRO-AMERICAN MUSIC.

For many years, black music was not taken seriously by white society. Racism and discrimination, particularly in the U.S.A., meant that the music did not reach a wider audience. Often it was "watered down" or presented as some sort of novelty item. The minstrel shows of the early twentieth century, for example, featured white musicians performing copies of black music. They would blacken their faces with burnt cork and imitate what they thought were black customs and speech. It is hardly surprising that white people gained a distorted view of black music from such shows. Fortunately, this situation gradually changed and Afro-American music is now receiving the respect and attention it deserves. Its influence upon other forms of music, ranging from Stravinsky to the Beatles, is also recognized.

The purpose of this book is to offer an introduction to some of the main forms of Afro-American music and to look at the social conditions which gave rise to them. Such a brief survey is bound to leave a lot out and, as Afro-American music is still developing, the book cannot cover all the latest trends. What it does try to do, however, is to highlight the African elements of the music and to illustrate the common heritage of musicians as diverse as Louis Armstrong, Bob Marley and James Brown.

For a long time, white audiences gained a distorted view of black music through the racist parodies of minstrel troupes such as the one shown here, in the 1920s.

PART ONE

AFRICAN MUSIC

A Scot, a Norwegian, a Greek and an Italian all have their own customs and traditions. They dress differently, eat different food and speak different languages. Despite these differences, however, they are all Europeans. We can talk about European styles of dress, European food and European music. Although the traditional music of Greece is different from that of Scotland, the two have strong similarities when compared to Indian or Chinese music. In the same way, when we talk about African music, we do not mean that all African music sounds the same. The traditional music of Nigeria is distinct from that of Zimbabwe or Zaire, for instance, but there are also certain common features. It is the common features of African music which we will be looking at in this section.

When listening to African music, it is important to remember that it is *African* and not European music. It has its own traditions and conventions about what is pleasing to the ear. For various historical and geographical reasons, however, African and European music have more in common than the music of Europe and that of Asia.

Nearly all African music shares the following important features. Try to bear them in mind when looking at what happened to the music when it was taken to the Americas.

Music occupies a central place in African life

In Africa there is music for every occasion. There are songs to be sung while bringing in the harvest or building a new house. There are songs to bring good luck and songs to keep away bad luck. Music is used as a means of maintaining law and order, with songs that pour scorn on wrongdoers and praise those deserving respect. Music also has a vital role to play in African religions.

So important is music in traditional African society, that some African languages do not have a separate word for it as it cannot be isolated from the activity which it accompanies.

African music does not have a passive audience

The European convention of an audience that sits and quietly listens to a musical performance would seem to be bad-mannered in traditional African society. Everyone joins in, by singing, playing an instrument, clapping or dancing. Music and dancing are seen as part of the same activity rather than one providing an accompaniment to the other. The CALL-AND-RESPONSE style, where one musician sings or plays a line and the others repeat or answer it, is common throughout Africa.

Rhythm is a very important element in African music

This does *not* mean that African music is nothing but drums. Percussion instruments are very important, however.

---

rhythm: *different combinations of stresses and sound lengths made into a pattern.*

---

gourd: *the fruit of a tropical plant, such as the calabash. When a gourd is dried, the seeds inside rattle when it is shaken.*

Percussion instruments are those which are banged, rattled or shaken. Besides drums, the list includes rattles, scrapers, bells, gongs and xylophones. African percussion instruments range from the huge wooden drums of the rain-forest to the gourd rattles of the grasslands or savanna. The most common form of percussive accompaniment throughout Africa, however, is hand-clapping.

There are also many African string and wind instruments and these too are played in a percussive way. The music is often built up of short phrases, regularly repeated to create a feeling of movement. This "creative repetition" is a common feature of African music.

The actual rhythms of African music are far more complex than those found in

This group of Angolan musicians, photographed about fifty years ago, display some of the vast number of musical instruments found in Africa. The large xylophones are the ancestor of the South American marimba. On the ground, in front of the musicians, you can see animal horn trumpets as well as drums, rattles and gongs. At the very front, it is possible to make out three thumb pianos – wooden boxes with thin strips of metal attached. The metal strips are plucked with the thumbs.

Europe. When a group of drummers are playing, for example, one instrument will produce a steady beat, or pulse, while the others play different rhythms on top of this. We use the word POLYRHYTHMIC to describe such a style of playing.

The "voice" of an instrument is important to African musicians

In traditional African belief, everything in

---

beat: *a regular pulse.*

nature has a soul or spirit. When you get a sound out of something you hear its "voice". This has two major effects on African music. Firstly, it means that anything which can be made to produce a sound can become a musical instrument. Secondly, it enables African musicians to adopt a far more individual approach to the playing of an instrument without the European restriction of a "right" or "wrong" tone.

African instruments are often used to imitate the human voice, the best-known example being the talking drums of West Africa. Instead of being rigid, the body of such a drum is made from thick strings of tough grass. The tension of the drum heads can be altered by squeezing the

Although there are parts of Africa where drums are rarely used, they are an important element in the music of West and Central Africa.

body of the drum. The tighter the heads, the higher the note produced; the looser the head, the lower the note. In this way it is possible to produce subtle variations in pitch which can be used to imitate human speech patterns.

African musicians have always experimented with ways of altering the "voice" of instruments. Sometimes strips of metal are attached to stringed instruments to produce a buzzing tone. The *hallam* is a stringed instrument in which the strings are stretched over a drum. When the strings are played, the drum vibrates – the ancestor of the banjo, an instrument introduced to America by Africans. European reed instruments, such as the oboe, also have their roots in Africa, where musicians first realized how to alter the tone of a flute by inserting a piece of stiff grass into the mouthpiece.

African singing imitates speech patterns

A "good" singer in Africa is one who can sound angry in an angry song, sad in a sad song, happy in a happy song, old in a song about old age and mocking in a song making fun of someone. Singing and acting are closely linked.

African singers like to "bend" notes, often sliding up to the first note of a phrase. They will sometimes shout words rather than singing them, and the use of falsetto is very common. (Falsetto is a register,

---

melody: *an arrangement of single notes. A tune.*

---

available to men's voices, above the normal pitch.)

A Muslim influence can be heard in the music of West Africa and also that of Spain

As the Spanish were the first Europeans to colonize land in the Americas and as many of the Africans taken there were from West Africa, this Muslim link is important.

The Arabs of North Africa travelled across the Sahara to trade with the great kingdoms of West Africa, long before Europeans ever went there. They introduced the Muslim religion – ISLAM – into the region. They traded not only in goods but in ideas, introducing new musical styles into West Africa, including elements of music from other countries they had conquered. In particular, the style of singing in Muslim areas of West Africa is closely related to Arab styles, especially the elaborate melody lines.

In Muslim parts of West Africa, there are professional musicians known as GRIOTS. Some griots specialize in providing songs for particular occasions – the birth of a child, for instance; others specialize in praise songs. Some are attached to a particular village or group of tradesmen, while others are wandering musicians. The griots have an important role as tellers of news and guardians of history.

The Arab influence also spread into Europe. The Moors of Morocco ruled southern Spain and Portugal for many years. They had a lasting influence upon the music of these areas, which is more rhythmically complex than music found elsewhere in Europe.

The Moors were finally pushed out of Spain in 1492, the same year that Christopher Columbus began the European conquest of the Americas.

PART TWO

AFRICAN MUSIC IN THE AMERICAS

"None of the African prisoners broke out into 'St. James's Infirmary' the minute the first of them was herded off the ship." (LeRoi Jones, *Blues People*, William Morrow, New York, 1963)
("St James's Infirmary" is the name of a famous blues song. See page 22.)

It is important to remember that the modern countries of Africa are largely a European invention, cutting across the boundaries of the old African kingdoms.

The Africans who were taken to the Americas came from the rain-forests in the west, the grasslands to the north, and from the Congo-Angola region.

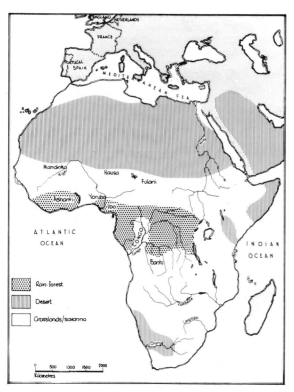

The American colonies in about 1770. ▶

The Africans who were taken to the Americas came from three main areas.

From the rain-forests of West Africa came the Yoruba, Ashanti and Ibo. The Muslim Hausa, Fulani and Mandinka lived in the grasslands to the north. From the Congo-Angola region on the coast of Central Africa came the Bantu. The British and French slave trade was centred upon West Africa, while the Spanish and Portuguese took Africans from Congo-Angola as well as buying them from the British. The Africans who were taken to the Americas were thus a mixture of many different peoples.

The situation was further complicated by the fact that the Europeans were constantly fighting amongst themselves and many of their colonies changed hands. Jamaica was taken from Spain by Britain, while St Lucia was alternately under French and British control. Haiti, part of the island of Hispaniola, was seized from Spain by France. Trinidad was a Spanish colony, managed by French colonists, which came under British control. In North America, the French colony of Louisiana was sold to the United States after the Americans had gained independence from Britain.

Often, one European power would free

rain-forest: *dense forest found in tropical areas where there is heavy rainfall.*

grasslands: *also known as savanna. Areas of open grass with scattered bushes and trees found in tropical areas where there is seasonal rainfall.*

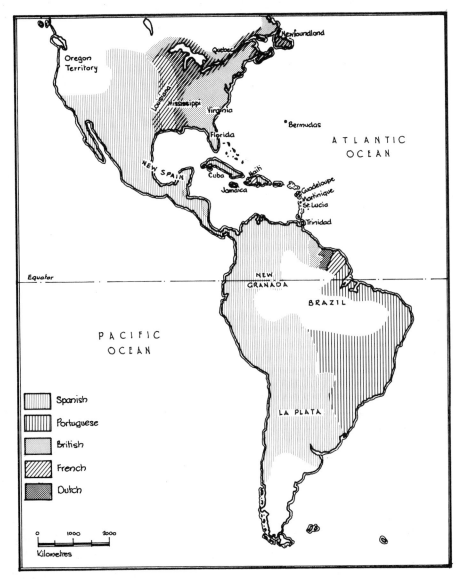

Oregon Territory
Quebec
Newfoundland
Louisiana
Mississippi
Virginia
Bermudas
Florida
NEW SPAIN
Cuba
Haiti
Jamaica
Guadeloupe
Martinique
St. Lucia
Trinidad
ATLANTIC OCEAN
NEW GRANADA
Equator
BRAZIL
PACIFIC OCEAN
LA PLATA

Spanish
Portuguese
British
French
Dutch

0   1000   2000
Kilometres

its slaves to help fight when it was attacked by another. The Spanish, for example, had freed their slaves in Jamaica when the island was attacked by the British. These freed slaves established the Maroon colonies in Jamaica, where they attempted to re-create their African lifestyle. The French freed their slaves in Louisiana when they were at war with Britain, creating the class of free blacks known as Creoles. In addition to this, Europeans would often move slaves from one colony to another.

The result of all this confusion was that Africans from different areas were mixed together and slowly lost their traditional cultural differences. So far as music was concerned, it was the common features which survived rather than the music of any one particular people. We refer to this as NEO-AFRICAN MUSIC (neo = new).

The three main forms of neo-African

Maroons: *the descendants of escaped slaves living in remote parts of Jamaica and Surinam. (From the Spanish word "cimarron", meaning "living in the mountains".)*

11

The Maroons of Jamaica gained their independence over two hundred years ago. The original copy of the independence treaty made in the reign of George II in 1738 is kept in Kingston. It gave the maroons the right to punish their own law-breakers and to pay no taxes to the British. This picture, taken in 1962, shows Colonel Walter Robertson, who was voted in as maroon chief in the 1930s.

music were music for dancing, work songs and religious music.

African dances

"When I came to Kingston, I was surprised to see the number of Africans

who were assembled together on Sundays . . . each different nation of Africa meet and dance after the nature of their own country. They still retain most of their native customs."
(From the memoirs of Equiano, an African who was a slave in Britain during the eighteenth century. After gaining his freedom, he travelled widely and wrote about what he saw.)

African dances have survived in many parts of the Americas. The rumba, the conga, the samba, the juba and the kalinda all have African roots. The traditional instruments used to accompany them have also survived, the most obvious being African-styled drums. The South American *marimba* is descended from the African xylophone. The thumb piano (a wooden soundbox with metal prongs fastened to it for the player to pluck with the thumbs) is common throughout Africa and reappeared in a larger form (made from a packing case) in the Caribbean. In Trinidad it is known as the box-bass, while in Jamaica it is the rumba-box.

The relationship between dancers and musicians kept to the African pattern, with neither being the servant of the other. Most dances followed the African tradition of ring dances. One or two dancers would be surrounded by a circle of singers and musicians. The call-and-response style of singing was generally used.

In some areas, plantation owners encouraged African dances, believing that they kept the slaves happy. Some went so far as to provide fiddles. Drums

marimba: *a South American xylophone. (The word "marimba" comes originally from West Africa.)*

plantation: *an estate in tropical countries where a crop such as cotton, tobacco or sugar is grown.*

were another matter, however. They could be used to pass on messages and the Europeans did all they could to stamp them out.

Work songs

"Without a song the bush-knife is dull."
(West African proverb)

Rhythmic songs to make work seem easier are not only found in Africa. What *is* African, however, is the use of songs related to the actual job being done. In European traditions this occurs only in sea-shanties and there is speculation that these were influenced by African and West Indian work songs.

In 1790, William Beckford wrote the following description of workers in a Jamaican sugar mill using call-and-response singing:

"When the mill is at work at night, there is something affecting in the songs of the women who feed it . . . sometimes you may hear one soft, complaining voice; and now a second and third chime in; and presently . . . a full chorus is heard to swell upon the ear, and then to die away again to the first original tune."
(*A Descriptive Account of the Island Jamaica*)

Often this call-and-response singing would follow the African pattern of unrhymed lines sung by one person, with a group answer after each line. In the following example, the first part of each line was sung by a solo singer. The response, which was sung by the other workers, is in brackets. "Norah" is the Biblical character Noah.

"Won't you ring old hammer? (Hammer ring)
Broke the handle in my hammer.
(Hammer ring)

13

Got to hammering in the Bible. (Hammer ring)
Got to talk about Norah. (Hammer ring)
Well God told Norah (Hammer ring)
You is a-going in the timber. (Hammer ring)"

Group work songs died out as machines did away with the need for gangs to work together. They survived well into this century, however, on the prison farms of the southern United States, where physical labour was part of the punishment.

Work songs were not always group efforts. Another form was the FIELD HOLLER.

Convicts in Mississippi clearing wreckage left by a tornado. This was probably some time in the 1940s.

This was sung by workers engaged on individual tasks. It usually consisted of one or two lines, often making use of falsetto singing. Many early hollers were sung in African dialect. In some, the singer would dwell upon personal hardships or the job in hand, while others were used as a way of keeping in touch with other solitary workers some distance away. (A falsetto voice will carry much further than one in the normal register.)

Alan Lomax, the American folk-song collector, travelled around the southern states before the Second World War tape-recording examples of work songs. This is what he said about field hollers:

"The lonely Negro workers piling up dirt on the levees, plowing in the cotton

fields, at work in the lonely mists of the riverbottoms . . . have poured their feelings into songs like these. The songs are addressed to the sun and the choking dust, to the stubborn mules, to the faithless woman of the night before, to the hard-driving captain; and they concern the essential loneliness of man on the earth."
(Quoted in *Black Music of Two Worlds* by John Storm Roberts, Praeger Publications Inc, 1972)

Religious music

African religions survived in many areas, though often several became mixed together, along with elements of Christianity. Shango, the Yoruba thunder god, was widely worshipped. There are still SHANGO cults in various parts of the Caribbean in which Shango is also identified with John the Baptist, while the Yoruba god of battle, Ogun, is linked with St Michael the Archangel. The drums used in these Shango cults are similar to those used by the Yoruba people.

KUMINA is a cult practised in eastern Jamaica. A Kumina ceremony consists of drumming, dancing, singing and possession by spirits. Two drums are used and the players sit on them in African fashion, using their heels to tighten the skin and change the pitch. Dancers circle around the drummers and move away when "possessed". The Kumina songs use call-and-response and include Bantu words.

VOUDON (Voodoo), formerly the state religion of Haiti, is also found in Martinique and Guadeloupe. It mixes Roman Catholicism with religious beliefs from Dahomey in West Africa. The Cuban cult,

LUCUMI, uses words from the Yoruba language, while the Jamaican word for a spell or charm, OBEAH, comes from *obia*, a word in the West African Ewe language.

Europeans were afraid that these neo-African cults would become the focus for rebellion and did all they could to stamp them out. They were particularly disturbed by drumming. One plantation owner said:

"Being Christmas Eve, our evening service was attended by most of our people. The glad tidings of great joy were heard with great attention. But scarcely was our worship closed, before the heathen negroes on the estate began to beat their drums, and to sing in the most outrageous manner. The noise lasted all night and prevented us from falling asleep.

After breakfast, I went down and

A dancer in a CANDOMBLE ceremony. Candomble is a neo-African religion of Brazil. Through hypnotic chants and dancing, the participants hope to achieve a trance-like state during which the gods can take possession of their bodies.

15

begged the negroes to desist, and expressed my surprise that having heard the word of God for so many years, they still continued their heathenish customs."

In Spanish, Portuguese and French colonies, the Africans were expected to adopt Roman Catholicism. In British colonies, the Church of England remained the religion of the wealthier whites, while the Africans came under the influence of the Non-Conformist sects, especially the Baptists. The music associated with black

---

sect: *a small group of people with a shared religious or political belief.*

Christianity is dealt with in more detail in Part Three.

*   *   *

In parts of the Americas where Africans formed the majority of the population, more of their music survived than in areas where they were in the minority. For this reason, the African elements in much Caribbean music are more obvious than those in the music of the U.S.A. On the other hand, the United States is a powerful country with world-wide influence, and forms of music developed there, such as blues, jazz and soul, are widely known. They have had a great impact on music in other parts of the world, including the Caribbean and Africa. We will therefore start by looking at black music in the U.S.A.

PART THREE

BLACK MUSIC IN THE U.S.A.

GOSPEL

Apart from the neo-African music mentioned in Part Two, gospel is the oldest form of black music in the United States. The term "gospel" was not used until the 1920s but the roots of this kind of music go back to the late eighteenth century when missionaries from the white Non-Conformist churches encouraged slaves to give up the African religions still followed by more than 90% of them. The word Non-Conformist is given to those Protestant churches in Britain which do not accept the authority of the Church of England. During the eighteenth and nineteenth centuries the Non-Conformists were often associated with movements for social change and suffered a great deal of hostility from those in authority.

Missionary work amongst slaves often met with similar hostility. Much of the white opposition to the slave trade had come from the Non-Conformist churches and plantation owners were worried that the missionaries would now encourage the slaves to revolt. The Church of England point of view was expressed by an eighteenth-century Archbishop of Canterbury who stated that even if a slave gave his soul to God, his body still belonged to his master. Many Christians felt that the social divisions in society had been created by God. The hymn "All Things Bright and Beautiful", written in 1848, has a verse, rarely sung nowadays, which illustrates this attitude:

> "The rich man in his castle,
> The poor man at his gate,
> God made them, high or lowly,
> And ordered their estate."

Many Baptists and Methodists who worked amongst the Africans did not accept that God had made them different. They would not only worship with slaves, but ate with them and generally treated them as equals in the sight of God. The plantation owners and the authorities saw this as a dangerous threat to the established order of things.

Many of those white people who campaigned against slavery did so as a result of their religious convictions. The most famous of these was the American, John Brown, who was hanged in 1859 after leading an unsuccessful rebellion of slaves at Harper's Ferry, Virginia. In many places, those in authority tried to stop black and white people worshipping together. The black churches which developed did not see social and religious issues as separate. They became more than just places of worship and there is a long tradition, in the Caribbean as well as the U.S.A., of black preachers who have also been community leaders.

African elements in black Christianity

One of the reasons that Non-Conformist sects found favour amongst the slaves was that their form of Christianity could be adapted to African traditions. Baptism of adults, for example, was similar to the

---

Baptists: *Christian sects that believe in the baptism of adults.*

Methodists: *Christian sects which follow the teachings of John Wesley (1703-91).*

---

water ceremonies found in parts of West Africa. The Non-Conformists also emphasized possession by the Holy Spirit, while many African religions were based on possession by the spirits of dead ancestors. We have already seen that possession is a feature of cults such as Kumina, and it is equally important in many black Christian sects. "Speaking in tongues" is a feature of several Non-Conformist sects. The "gift of tongues", the ability to speak in foreign or unknown languages, was given to the disciples of Jesus at Pentecost (Whitsun). Something similar is also an element in several neo-African cults, where African words, the meaning of which has been long forgotten, are used at the emotional climax of ceremonies.

Dancing is central to many African religions but the Christian church regarded it as sinful. The answer was the RING SHOUT, which existed in black churches well into this century. "Shout" comes from an African word, *saut*, meaning a religious dance. A ring shout consisted of a circle of worshippers moving in single file, singing and stamping their feet. The tempo built up slowly until possession by the Holy Ghost took place. (Compare this with the Kumina cult of Jamaica.) Another way around the ban on dancing was to sway the body from side to side without actually moving the feet.

The development of gospel music

Music has always been a vital part of black Christianity. Following emancipation (the ending of slavery), black people were not allowed to preach a sermon in some parts of the United States. Singing took its place. The leader of a meeting would sing a line, the congregation would repeat or answer it, in call-and-response style. The congregation also joined in by clapping, stamping or swaying. This form of sermon has remained a feature of black worship. It often starts quietly, with the preacher speaking. Gradually it develops into a rhythmic chant, the responses from the congregation becoming louder and more frequent. Often the preacher will strike the pulpit to emphasize the rhythm. At the climax, the piano or organ and choir join in and the chant becomes a song.

Religious music has also been used as a form of rebellion.

"Way over in Egypt's land
We will gain the victory
The Lord will set his people free
We will gain the day."

SPIRITUALS, as such songs were known, worked on two levels. Taken at face value, the above example is about the Israelites held captive in Egypt. It also expresses, however, a cry for freedom. Spirituals are full of references to "crossing Jordan's river", "returning to Zion" or the Lord "setting his people free". Black people held captive in the Americas used such songs as a way of singing about their own lives and their hopes for a better world. The custom of "hiding" messages in songs is still common in Africa. A recent example is the CHIMURENGA music of Zimbabwe (see Part Six).

The words of gospel songs have always related to everyday life. Old Testament prophets feature as real people, not as something remote, from the past. Again, this reflects African tradition, where dead ancestors are believed to still take an active interest in the well-being of the living. A large number of songs take images from the world around them, such as the recurring theme of the "gospel train" or the telephone as in "get me Jesus on the line". Others refer to issues like unemployment, poverty and war.

---

spirituals: *religious songs developed by black people in the southern United States.*

Zion: *the hill on which Jerusalem stands. Also used as another name for Heaven.*

Jordan: *a river in Israel.*

The gospel singer *MAHALIA JACKSON*. She was born in New Orleans in 1911. Her parents tried to shield her from the "sinful" music of that city, but she heard recordings by Bessie Smith on a neighbour's gramophone. Her vocal style owed much to the great blues singer, though the content of her songs was very different. A few gospel singers performed blues songs as well, but Mahalia Jackson never did. As she once said, "A blues singer has a broken spirit and is burdened."

Gospel music has never been confined to churches. As long ago as 1870, THE FISK JUBILEE SINGERS made a concert tour of the United States and Britain. Street evangelists, usually accompanying themselves on guitar, became common in the

---

evangelist: *a preacher.*

19

Unfortunate Rake", for example, provided the basis for the cowboy song, "Streets of Laredo", and the blues, "St James's Infirmary". Other well-known examples of ballad blues are "Frankie and Johnny", "Stag-o-Lee" and "Stewball". Many of these songs concerned characters in trouble with the law. "Stag-o-Lee" (sometimes called Stack Lee) killed a man called Billy Lyons for stealing his new Stetson hat. "Frankie and Johnny" (also known as "Frankie and Albert") is the tale of a woman who shoots her man "because he done her wrong".

Other songs refer to current events. "Good Whiskey Blues" was written by PETIE WHEATSTRAW to celebrate the end of Prohibition (an American law, repealed in 1933, which banned the sale of alcohol). BROWNIE McGHEE's "Million Lonesome Women" was composed during the Second World War, while "Vietcong Blues" was a protest against the Vietnam War by JUNIOR WELLS. The vast majority of blues songs, however, concern the relationship between the sexes, about which they are often very frank:

"You're good looking but you got to die someday
Better give me some loving before you pass away."

Sexual boasting is common, often disguised by the use of fairly obvious double meanings:

"I'm your ice-cream man
Stop me when I'm passing by."

"I don't care what the people think
I'm gonna put a tiger in your tank."

It should not be assumed that all blues songs were sad. Even when they dealt with hardship, they often treated it with a certain resigned humour:

"Ashes to ashes and dust to dust
If the whiskey don't get you then the cocaine must."

It is not clear when it became common to use the description "blues" for a particular form of music, but we do know that W.C. HANDY composed his "Memphis Blues" in 1912, followed in 1914 by his most famous song, "St Louis Blues". Handy is often referred to as the "Father of the Blues". Like most such titles, this is an exaggeration, but he certainly brought the blues to a wider audience. He was a bandleader and composer and his compositions follow the pattern found in military band marches and the ragtime

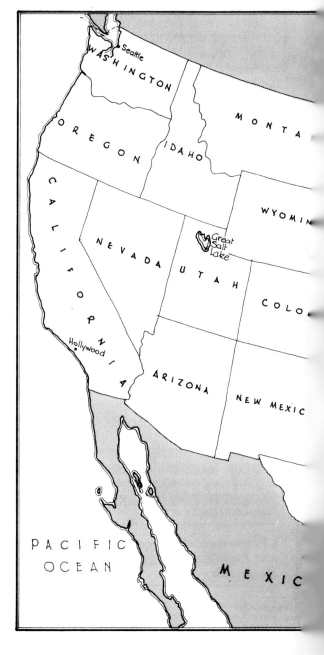

The gospel singer *MAHALIA JACKSON. She was born in New Orleans in 1911. Her parents tried to shield her from the "sinful" music of that city, but she heard recordings by Bessie Smith on a neighbour's gramophone. Her vocal style owed much to the great blues singer, though the content of her songs was very different. A few gospel singers performed blues songs as well, but Mahalia Jackson never did. As she once said, "A blues singer has a broken spirit and is burdened."*

Gospel music has never been confined to churches. As long ago as 1870, THE FISK JUBILEE SINGERS made a concert tour of the United States and Britain. Street evangelists, usually accompanying themselves on guitar, became common in the

---

evangelist: *a preacher.*

19

1920s. Sometimes they performed in twos, and fine examples of this kind of gospel duet can be heard in the recordings of SISTER ROSETTA THARPE and MARIE KNIGHT. Their music can perhaps best be described as "religious rock'n'roll" (though, of course, the term rock'n'roll did not come into use until later).

Most recorded gospel music was performed by trained groups of singers known as gospel quartets. (They were called quartets even when they contained more than four members.) Among the best-known were THE DIXIE HUMMINGBIRDS and THE FIVE BLIND BOYS. They had a close harmony style of singing, rather like that of barbershop quartets, but also used call-and-response delivery. These quartets were very popular and their influence can be heard in black vocal group music ranging from THE INK SPOTS in the 1940s to the TAMLA MOTOWN groups of the 'sixties.

A more emotionally intense form of delivery was adopted by singers such as MAHALIA JACKSON. Known as the "surge" style, it used long, decorative melody lines and dramatic changes in volume. Again, this style has had an influence on black popular music, particularly the recordings of RAY CHARLES.

Gospel music has adopted a variety of musical styles over the years, but there have been several unifying factors. These include the use of call-and-response, an emphasis upon rhythm, and passionate delivery. Gospel's influence upon other forms of black music has been enormous, especially in the development of soul music.

THE BLUES

If gospel is the religious music of the black people of the U.S.A., then the blues is their folk music. The music retained many African elements, particularly in Mississippi, where blacks outnumbered whites by three to one.

Vocal styles

Falsetto singing is common in the blues, as is the use of a yodel in the middle of a line. Singers often adopted a vocal style which followed speech patterns. Most important of all, however, is the habit of bending notes or sliding up to the first note of a phrase. This technique, which is also used by blues guitarists and harmonica players, gave rise to what are known as BLUE NOTES. These replace the third, seventh and, sometimes, fifth notes of the European major scale. In the key of G major, for example, the third degree of the scale is B, but a blues singer might use B flat or slide from B flat to B. Often, a tune will end on a flattened seventh. It is this which gives the blues its particular plaintive quality, with tunes that are neither wholly in a major nor in a minor key. Some people have argued that there is actually a "blues scale", derived from African scales, but the use of blue notes does not follow any formal convention.

Instrumental styles

The blues grew out of field hollers (see page 14) and was originally an unaccompanied vocal music. Instrumental blues often attempt to imitate the human voice. This is particularly true of the harmonica, or "blues harp", which, in the hands of an artist like SONNY BOY WILLIAMSON, took on a tone of haunting sadness. Confusingly, there were two blues harp players called Sonny Boy Williamson. The original, John Lee Williamson, was murdered in 1948 when he was only thirty-four. Another musician, Rice Miller, adopted the name and became equally famous. This second Sonny Boy Williamson died in 1965. Blues guitarists developed a technique of sliding a knife or the neck of a bottle along the strings of their instrument, to produce a

vocal: *produced by the voice.*

singing tone. A more modern alternative to this "bottleneck" style is to use a metal ring worn around the little finger.

The guitar and harmonica are often used to answer the singer in a call-and-response manner. For an artist such as B.B. KING, who has been recording since 1949, the guitar is an extension of his own voice, expressing emotions which he cannot put into words.

Traditional blues guitar styles owed much to West African traditions. In fact, the earliest accompanied blues songs made use of the banjo, which originated in Africa. Guitars were played percussively, the frame often doubling as a drum. The use of short, repeated, rhythmic patterns was common. Although modern blues guitarists have tended to adopt a more melodic style, the older technique can still be heard in the electric guitar playing of JOHN LEE HOOKER in the 1960s.

The development of the blues

The earliest blues songs followed the very free form of field hollers, but gradually a more fixed pattern emerged, the so-called TWELVE BAR BLUES. This is based on the I, IV and V chords of European harmony and consists of twelve bars divided into three lines of four bars each. The first half of each line is sung, the second half is an "answer" played on one of the accompanying instruments. The first two lines are usually the same or very similar, while the third line rhymes with the first and completes the phrase. For example:

---

chord: *a combination of notes sounded at the same time.*

---

harmony: *a system of arranging combinations of notes. Since the seventeenth century, European harmony has been based around major and minor scales.*

I, IV and V chords: *the chords based on the first, fourth and fifth degrees of a major or minor scale.*

C ///	C ///	C ///	C ///
F ///	F ///	C ///	C ///
G ///	F ///	C ///	C ///

The chords of a simple twelve-bar blues.

A more complex variation.

C ///	F7 ///	C ///	C7 ///
F ///	F7 ///	C ///	C7 ///
Dm ///	G7 ///	C ///	C ///

"Michigan water tastes like sherry wine
(two bars plus two bars instrumental)
Michigan water tastes like sherry wine
(as above)
I'm gwine back to Michigan, to the one I left behind."
(as above)

Those lines, first heard in Texas in the early years of this century, reappeared in a rather different form in Chicago in the late 'sixties:

"I think I'll move back south, where the
          water tastes like sherry wine,
Think I'll move back south, where the
          water's sweet as sherry wine,
This Lake Michigan water tastes to me
          just like turpentine."
(Buddy Guy, "A Man and the Blues")

This illustrates another feature of the blues, the existence of a shared store of lyrics. Blues musicians have always felt free to borrow from this common source. The blues expresses personal feelings which are understood by a wider community. It is this shared experience which is important rather than the notion of "originality".

British and Irish ballads, taken to the Americas by eighteenth-century immigrants, also found their way into the store of blues lyrics. The Irish ballad, "The

Unfortunate Rake", for example, provided the basis for the cowboy song, "Streets of Laredo", and the blues, "St James's Infirmary". Other well-known examples of ballad blues are "Frankie and Johnny", "Stag-o-Lee" and "Stewball". Many of these songs concerned characters in trouble with the law. "Stag-o-Lee" (sometimes called Stack Lee) killed a man called Billy Lyons for stealing his new Stetson hat. "Frankie and Johnny" (also known as "Frankie and Albert") is the tale of a woman who shoots her man "because he done her wrong".

Other songs refer to current events. "Good Whiskey Blues" was written by PETIE WHEATSTRAW to celebrate the end of Prohibition (an American law, repealed in 1933, which banned the sale of alcohol). BROWNIE McGHEE's "Million Lonesome Women" was composed during the Second World War, while "Vietcong Blues" was a protest against the Vietnam War by JUNIOR WELLS. The vast majority of blues songs, however, concern the relationship between the sexes, about which they are often very frank:

"You're good looking but you got to die
someday
Better give me some loving before you
pass away."

Sexual boasting is common, often disguised by the use of fairly obvious double meanings:

"I'm your ice-cream man
Stop me when I'm passing by."

"I don't care what the people think
I'm gonna put a tiger in your tank."

It should not be assumed that all blues songs were sad. Even when they dealt with hardship, they often treated it with a certain resigned humour:

"Ashes to ashes and dust to dust
If the whiskey don't get you then the
cocaine must."

It is not clear when it became common to use the description "blues" for a particular form of music, but we do know that W.C. HANDY composed his "Memphis Blues" in 1912, followed in 1914 by his most famous song, "St Louis Blues". Handy is often referred to as the "Father of the Blues". Like most such titles, this is an exaggeration, but he certainly brought the blues to a wider audience. He was a bandleader and composer and his compositions follow the pattern found in military band marches and the ragtime

pieces of Scott Joplin, with an introduction followed by several different sections. The

themes which he used, however, were all adapted from blues songs which he had heard.

In the 1920s the first recordings of the blues were made. It is from this point that we can more accurately trace the development of the music. By this time, the blues could be divided into two main types, country and city.

ragtime: *a piano style which was developed in the southern United States during the late nineteenth century. It combined a regular "oom pah" left-hand part with a syncopated right-hand melody. (Ragtime is short for "ragged time".)*

syncopated: *describes music in which the accent (or stress) is not placed on the regular strong beat.*

Country blues

This was the older style, performed in rural

The U.S.A.

Inside a sharecropper's home in Missouri, 1938.

areas of Mississippi and Texas. Racism, particularly in Mississippi, was widespread and the majority of black people were trapped by the system known as sharecropping. Under this system, a black farmer bought his seed and other equipment from his white landlord. It was bought on account, the loan, plus interest, being paid back at harvest time. In effect, this meant that black farmers were never out of debt and their freedom was severely limited.

The Mississippi Delta, a D-shaped area of lowland between the Mississippi and Yazoo rivers, was the home of the most famous country blues musicians. To become a wandering singer was one way of escaping the virtual slavery of work on the land. The Delta blues style was characterized by a strong African element and a very intense form of delivery. It reached its artistic peak in the music of ROBERT JOHNSON. He recorded only about thirty tracks but these were enough to make his reputation as the "King of the Delta Blues Singers". A notorious womanizer, he was poisoned by a jealous girlfriend in 1937, at the age of only twenty-one.

In Texas, where conditions for black people were not as harsh, a more relaxed style developed. BLIND LEMON JEFFERSON was one of the first country blues artists to

BLIND LEMON JEFFERSON.

25

be recorded, making records in Chicago between 1925 and 1930. He was found frozen to death in a snowstorm after the last of these sessions.

kazoo: *a cigar-shaped metal instrument which works on the same principle as the comb-and-tissue-paper. (Place a thin piece of tissue paper around a comb, hold it close to your mouth and hum.)*

washboard: *a corrugated metal sheet used for scrubbing clothes. This can be used as a percussion instrument by putting metal thimbles on the fingers and scraping them up and down the board.*

Not all country blues was played by solo musicians. JUG BANDS were a popular form of entertainment also. They used simple instruments such as kazoos, washboards, fiddles and guitars. A piano would sometimes be added and the bass was produced by a musician blowing across the neck of a stone whiskey jug – hence the name, jug band. The use of washboard and jug followed in the African tradition that anything which produced a sound could become a musical instrument. Bands such as THE MISSISSIPPI JOOK BAND, GUS CANNON'S JUG STOMPERS and THE MEMPHIS JUG BAND played dance tunes as well as blues. The Memphis Jug Band also featured on many early gospel records.

One form of country blues remained restricted to a single area, the isolated swampland of the Louisiana Bayou. Louisiana had been a French colony and after the British defeated the French in Canada in 1763, many French Canadians settled there. They were known as CAJUNS (from the French name for Canada, Arcadia). Cajun folk music features the piano accordion, and black inhabitants of the region adopted the instrument too, using it to play the blues. The resultant music became known as ZYDECO and it is still performed in a mixture of English and French.

City blues

This was the style, also known as CLASSIC BLUES, which developed in the music halls of Chicago and New York. It was the first form of blues to be recorded and most of the famous singers were women. The greatest of them all was BESSIE SMITH, the "Empress of the Blues". Born in 1898 in Chattanooga, Tennessee, she began her career singing in the tent shows, travelling variety companies that toured the United States, performing in areas where there were no permanent theatres. Many jazz and blues musicians gained their first professional experience in such shows. Bessie Smith made her first recordings in 1923 and they are arguably the finest examples of the blues on record. The suffering of her private life was poured into her music, which had great emotional impact. She died in a car crash in Mississippi in 1937.

"Bessie Smith" was a fabulous deal to watch . . . she dominated a stage. You didn't turn your head when she went on. You just watched Bessie. . . . When she was performing, you could hear a pin drop."
(Danny Barker, quoted in *Hear Me Talkin' To Ya*, edited by Nat Shapiro and Nat Hentoff, Rinehart & Co. Inc., New York, 1955)

The classic blues singers were usually accompanied by a piano or a small jazz band, featuring musicians such as the young LOUIS ARMSTRONG. Their songs were not all blues in the strictest sense, but whatever they sang was delivered in a blues style.

Later urban blues styles . . .

During the Depression of the 1930s, thousands of black people migrated to the cities, looking for work. A new, urban style of blues developed in which boogie woogie pianists and small blues bands played an important role.

. . . Boogie woogie

In the late 'thirties and early 'forties, "boogie woogie fever" swept America, inspired by the brilliant trio made up by the pianists JIMMY YANCEY, MEADE LUX LEWIS and PETE JOHNSON.

Boogie woogie had developed in the segregated drinking clubs or "barrel houses" of the south. In order to be heard above the noise, barrel-house pianists used a driving, rhythmic style of playing. The left hand pounded out a pattern of repeated phrases, on top of which the right hand executed complicated variations, using triplets to contrast with the duple time of the bass. The roots of this style can be traced back to West African xylophone techniques. (The great boogie woogie pianist MEMPHIS SLIM made some recordings in the 'sixties using a celeste rather than a piano, making the similarities even more obvious.)

In Chicago, boogie woogie pianists became the main attraction at "house rent parties". As the name implies, these were parties held to raise money to pay the rent.

Segregation was enforced by law in many parts of the United States. (Notice the police order on the left side of the building.) This particular picture was taken in Belle Glade, Florida, in 1945. It was in such drinking houses that boogie woogie was born.

Guests paid an entrance fee, while the host provided the drinks and the pianist.

...Blues bands

The earliest blues bands displayed a strong jazz influence. In Chicago, BIG BILL BROONZY formed a band which included trumpet, clarinet and bass. In Kansas City, blues and jazz had always been closely linked. The COUNT BASIE ORCHESTRA, for example, was known as "the band that plays the blues". Kansas City musicians had a great influence on the "jump blues" style which developed on the West Coast, featuring boogie woogie piano and wild saxophone playing. The West Coast became an important blues centre during the Second World War, as many black people migrated there from Texas to work in the armaments factories. It was there that T-BONE WALKER developed the use of the electric guitar. His style was jazz-influenced, using the sustaining qualities of the instrument to play flowing, melodic lines.

...Chicago blues

During the 'fifties a new Chicago style

Buildings like the one here would still have ▶ been in use in the 'fifties, particularly for migrants from the rural south.

28

replaced the one developed by Big Bill Broonzy. It was more aggressive and the music produced by artists such as MUDDY WATERS and HOWLING WOLF was a heavily amplified version of the old Mississippi Delta blues. ELMORE JAMES took the country "bottleneck" style and adapted it to suit the electric guitar, his recordings being characterized by the generous use of echo. Harmonica players developed the technique of playing with their hands cupped around a microphone.

The music centred around the bars of Chicago's Southside district.

"Inside it's crowded and the music clamours against the narrow walls over the heads of the dancers milling in front of the bandstand. The guitar player and the drummer stay on the stand, but a harp player from the neighbourhood pulls the microphone cord as far as it will go and sits at a table besides his girl, blowing the blues for her over the din."
(Samuel Charters describing a Southside bar in the early 'sixties. Sleevenote to the Vanguard album "Chicago/The Blues/Today")

Rhythm and blues

American record companies had a policy of releasing black music on different labels from their white artists. Records aimed at the black market were known as "Race Records". During the 'forties and 'fifties the term "Rhythm and Blues" was introduced

instead. This covered everything from the jump blues of LOUIS JORDAN to the guitar shuffle of CHUCK BERRY and the harmony vocals of THE INK SPOTS. In the 1950s, this music was introduced to a wider teenage audience by the white disc jockey ALAN FREED. He called the music ROCK'N'ROLL.

By the mid-1960s most blues musicians found that they had a far larger audience amongst white teenagers than black. The earliest albums of groups such as THE BEATLES and THE ROLLING STONES contained almost exact copies of records by black artists, many of them previously unknown to white audiences in both Britain and the U.S.A. The Stones recorded four tracks at the Chess studios in Chicago, with the blues musician MUDDY WATERS reputedly playing rhythm guitar. Several other blues artists, among them SONNY BOY WILLIAMSON and JOHN LEE HOOKER, recorded with white rock bands. In Britain, JOHN MAYALL and ERIC CLAPTON introduced the blues to a whole new audience. Clapton, one of the most idolized of rock guitarists, had this to say about the influences on his playing:

> "At first I played exactly like Chuck Berry . . . then I got into older bluesmen. . . . I dug Big Bill Broonzy; then I heard a lot of cats I had never heard of before like Robert Johnson. Later I turned on to B.B. King and it's been that way ever since."
> (B. Cook, *Listen To The Blues*, Robson Books, 1975)

For others, commercial success came too late. In the late 'sixties, CREAM, one of the best-known of all rock groups, recorded a song written by the blues musician SKIP JAMES. The song was "I'm So Glad" and James' share of the royalties from the record came just in time to pay for his funeral.

The decline of the blues

At the same time as the blues was becoming popular with white teenagers,

The 'sixties were the years of Black Power and the Civil Rights movement. The picture on the right shows police in action during the Watts Riots. The rioting in Watts, the predominantly black area of Los Angeles, was repeated in other American cities throughout the 'sixties. The photograph below shows a young Black Muslim at a street meeting. The Muslims argued that Christianity was imposed upon black people by slave owners and that their true religion was Islam. Many adopted Islamic names, the boxer Muhammed Ali being the most well-known example, while others used the letter X to symbolize the African name which had been stolen from them.

30

for young black people born in the cities it was already becoming something of an embarrassment. "Harps, moaning . . . shit like that," was how one described it. They turned at first to the smoother style of B.B. KING. King, who came from Memphis, used saxophones and trumpets in his band as well as piano, bass and drums. His own guitar style was influenced by that of T-Bone Walker and was in turn to influence not only the younger generation of Chicago guitarists but also white rock musicians such as Eric Clapton.

The 'sixties were the years of the Civil Rights Movement and Black Power. The blues, with its songs of cotton farming,

poverty, broken love affairs, drinking and gambling, seemed out of place in the America of MARTIN LUTHER KING and MALCOLM X. A new style developed, one which took much of its inspiration from gospel music. It became known as SOUL.

SOUL

One of the first singers successfully to mix gospel-style music with non-religious lyrics was RAY CHARLES. Born in Albany, Georgia, in 1930, he lost his sight through glaucoma shortly after his sixth birthday.

When he was older, he moved to Seattle, where he got a job as a "cocktail pianist", playing background music in clubs. He then joined the backing band of the blues guitarist LOWELL FULSON. In 1953, he won a recording contract of his own with Atlantic Records and it was in his third recording session that the song "I've Got A Woman" revealed the musical direction he was to

RAY CHARLES in the 1950s.

take. The blues singer Big Bill Broonzy was moved to complain, "He's crying, sanctified. He's mixing the blues with the spirituals. He should be singing in a church."

The vocal style that Broonzy spoke of was indeed like that of a preacher, urging the audience (congregation) to join in, repeating lines over and over, his voice moving from a low rasp to a falsetto shriek. Many of his lyrics were borrowed or adapted from gospel songs. For example, "This Little Light Of Mine" became "This Little Girl Of Mine", while "Nobody But You, Lord" was shortened to "Nobody But You". The addition of a female vocal group, THE RAELETTES, emphasized the gospel sound with their use of call-and-response.

In the early 'sixties, Ray Charles changed direction, concentrating on country and western songs and popular ballads. Even amidst the lush string arrangement of a song like "Georgia On My Mind", however, the gospel-inspired voice is in evidence. The development of soul music, meanwhile, was taken up by one of the most influential figures in the history of black music, JAMES BROWN. He pioneered what were to be the main ingredients of soul music for the next two decades: chattering guitars, broken bass patterns, horn riffs and gospel-style singing. Rhythm became increasingly more important than melody. In long numbers, the backing band would repeat short rhythmic phrases (riffs) while Brown improvised vocals. The steady "walking bass" which had been a characteristic of much black music since the 'twenties, was abandoned for a syncopated style made up of separated clusters of notes. The guitarists played their instruments with the strings held tight, to produce a scratching tone. Brown kept a tight hold on the band. They were rehearsed to perfection and musicians were reputedly fined for playing

---

country and western: *the white folk music of the south-eastern U.S.A.*

---

ballad: *a slow, sentimental song.*

"walking bass": *a jazz bass accompaniment consisting of medium-tempo ascending and descending notes. (For example, in the key of C Major, C, E, G, A, C, A, G, E, C.)*

---

wrong notes. The act was too expansive to be captured adequately in the three minutes of a single record (these were the days before the twelve-inch disco mix), but the album "The James Brown Show Live At The Apollo" remained in the *Billboard* chart for over a year. (*Billboard* is an American music paper.)

Unlike many musicians, whose style becomes more mellow with age and fame, Brown did nothing to soften his musical approach. Songs such as "Say It Loud, I'm Black And I'm Proud" earned him the title "Soul Brother Number One". So great was his influence on black teenagers that an unscheduled television appearance of his was enough to stop an outbreak of inner-city rioting.

During the 'sixties, the word "soul" came to cover a variety of styles, the extremes of which can be heard in the releases of the record companies ATLANTIC and TAMLA MOTOWN.

Atlantic

Although based in New York, Atlantic was noted for its recordings of the intense southern style of soul music, sometimes known as "deep soul". This mixed blues and gospel in almost equal measures. Trumpets and saxophones were used to imitate the role of the choir in gospel music, while a gospel-style organ was a feature of many records.

From 1960, Atlantic also released the records made at the STAX studio in Memphis. Stax was one of the many small American record companies which relied on the majors for national promotion and distribution. Situated on the Mississippi, midway between New Orleans and Chicago, Memphis had always been a musical melting pot. It was here that B.B. King and Elvis Presley developed their respective styles. There was much sharing of ideas between black and white musicians, and the Stax houseband, BOOKER T AND THE M.G.S, was a racially mixed group. They provided the backing for Stax/Atlantic stars such as OTIS REDDING, WILSON PICKETT and SAM AND DAVE as well as recording in their own right.

Following a dispute with Stax, Atlantic switched to another influential southern studio, MUSCLE SHOALS in Alabama. It was here that the most successful woman soul singer, ARETHA FRANKLIN, made her first recordings for Atlantic. Her roots were firmly in gospel music, her father, C.L. Franklin, having been a famous preacher. Enormous hits with "I Never Loved A Man (The Way I Loved You)", "Respect" and "Natural Woman" won her the title "Soul Sister Number One". As with James Brown, her talent enabled her to survive changes of fashion in the 'seventies and she remains a dominant figure in black music.

Tamla Motown

Tamla Motown, based in Detroit, represented the other extreme of 'sixties soul music. Unashamedly commercial, it aimed at an international pop market, becoming the most successful black record company ever.

In 1960, BERRY GORDY formed a record label which he called Tammie, soon to be changed to Tamla. The first Tamla releases were in the doo wop style. This was a form of black vocal group music, heavily gospel-influenced, which had a lot of success in the rock'n'roll market. Doo wop groups were the first black artists to appear regularly on television. With their neat dress and clean-cut image they were seen as much less of a threat than wilder black artists such as LITTLE RICHARD. Tamla had a hit with "Shop Around" by THE MIRACLES and Gordy set up another company, which he called Motown. (Detroit was the centre of the American car industry and Motown was a shortened form of "motor town".) Gordy started buying out other small Detroit record labels and adding their artists to his roster. He also started to use the song-writing talents of BRIAN and EDDIE HOLLAND and LAMONT DOZIER. Between 1962 and 1966, Tamla Motown artists such as THE SUPREMES, THE FOUR TOPS, MARTHA AND THE VANDELLAS, STEVIE WONDER and THE TEMPTATIONS had a string of hit records on both sides of the Atlantic.

The Motown sound was the product of a musical production line. The backing musicians were largely anonymous and had no chance to record their own material. Gordy kept a tight grip on his artists, not only choosing their material for them but also dictating their style of dress. As he said of The Supremes:

"We had some trouble with them at first. You must be very strict with young artists."
(*Rolling Stone* magazine, U.S.A.)

Motown produced some of the best dance music of the 'sixties, but gradually the strains within the "family" began to show. In 1967, the song-writing team of Holland-Dozier-Holland left. In 1971, Stevie Wonder and Marvin Gaye negotiated new deals giving them artistic freedom. In the same year, the company moved from Detroit to Hollywood so that Gordy could concentrate upon the developing film career of DIANA ROSS. By 1975, THE JACKSON FIVE and THE FOUR TOPS had left Motown.

Motown retained the rights to the name "The Jackson Five" (and the label also retained one of the brothers, Jermaine, who had married Berry Gordy's daughter). The other brothers moved to EPIC RECORDS, where they recorded as THE JACKSONS. Gradually, the solo efforts of MICHAEL JACKSON became more important than the group, a process which culminated in the success of his 1979 album, "Off The Wall". This album was a result of Jackson's partnership with the veteran jazz producer QUINCY JONES. It yielded four top-ten singles and was followed a few years later by the even more successful "Thriller" album.

Motown, meanwhile, retained the rights

Motown groups such as THE SUPREMES were encouraged to adopt a style of dress which appealed to as wide an audience as possible.

Funk

"Free Your Mind and Your Ass Will Follow."

to older Jackson Five material, which they continued to repackage, giving Michael Jackson two more top-ten hits with records which had not done well on their original release. The days when Tamla Motown dominated black popular music, however, were over. During the 'seventies, the label was pushed into second place by the smooth PHILADELPHIA sound of THE O'JAYS and BILLY PAUL. It continued to have success with THE COMMODORES and RICK JAMES, though, and expanded into films as well as music.

Not all soul music in the 'seventies was of this commercial variety. The word "funk" was used to describe the more aggressive style which took James Brown as its model.

In the late 'sixties, SLY STONE had mixed soul with elements of white rock music and an extravagant stage show. His experiments were continued in the 'seventies by GEORGE CLINTON whose declared aim was "to rescue dance music from the blahs". He formed a variety of groups, PARLIAMENT, FUNKADELIC, BOOTSY'S RUBBER BAND, BRIDES OF FUNKENSTEIN, often sharing the same members and existing at the same time as each other. Clinton took on the role of Doctor Funkenstein, dedicated to creating "one nation under a groove".

Clinton's greatest rivals were, EARTH, WIND AND FIRE, who had a more jazz-based approach. Whereas Clinton's stage act made humorous use of science-fiction and horror movies, Earth, Wind and Fire showed a more serious interest in Egyptian mythology and mystic religions. What they, and other funk bands, shared was the fact that their music could not be contained within a three-minute record. The twelve-inch single was developed to solve this problem, aimed primarily at the disco market rather than the charts.

Hip hop

Although the word soul had referred to a specific style of music in the 'sixties, it gradually came to be a general term for black popular music, in the way that rhythm and blues had been in the 'fifties.

GEORGE CLINTON plans his next move.

Some spectacular break-dancing.

The popular styles vary from city to city, each with a sub-culture of its own. In Washington D.C., there is a form of music known as GO-GO. This takes its inspiration from the hard-edged funk of James Brown. It is essentially live music, the best bands being those that can keep the most dancers on the floor for the longest time. Chicago's HOUSE music, on the other hand, is the creation of disc jockeys. D.J.s such as FARLEY JACKMASTER FUNK are the influence behind a style which borrows freely from other forms of soul and disco but which mixes them in its own distinctive way.

The most widely known modern black urban style, however, is HIP HOP, which developed in the South Bronx district of New York. One of the main features of the hip hop scene is the rapidity with which fashions change. It is very much a "street" music, developing almost week by week. For this reason, it is only possible to make general points about the style.

Although it is the latest form of black music, it has its roots firmly in other Afro-American styles and, whether deliberately or not, has strong links with African music. The term hip hop does not refer only to music, but also to dancing (breaking and body-popping), poetry (rapping) and graffiti art. These elements are not seen as separate activities but complement each other.

Break-dancing is in the tradition of competitive, largely male, dancing which

37

stretches back to neo-African dances such as the juba and the kalinda. In the juba, for example, a large circle would be formed with one dancer in the middle performing complicated steps. When exhausted, he would be replaced by another dancer.

"Juba jump an' Juba sing
Juba cut that pigeon's wing,
Juba whirl that foot about,
Juba blow that candle out."

Rapping, a form of rhythmic, generally improvised poetry using rhyming couplets, echoes the praise and mocking songs of West Africa. Rappers like to praise themselves or their "crew" while pouring scorn on the puny efforts of their rivals. Often one record will answer the charges made in another and a recorded argument might develop, as happened in 1985 when there was a whole series of "Roxanne" records. Similar traditions exist in both calypso and reggae, as we will see later. Rappers also deal with social issues, such as drug abuse and unemployment. One of the pioneers of hip hop, AFRIKA BAMBAATAA, saw it as a way of channelling the energies wasted in inter-gang fighting.

Like other forms of Afro-American music, hip hop borrows freely from other sources, adapting them to its own ends. Scratching, for instance, involves moving the stylus back and forth across the surface of a record to produce a rhythmic effect. The use of two turntables ("wheels of steel") is common, the operator switching from one record to another or mixing the two together. Electro reduces dance music to its barest framework, concentrating on short, repeated phrases. The use of electronic gadgetry, such as synthesizers and drum machines, is common, but the so-called "human beatboxes" have developed the skill of achieving similar effects with their mouths and a microphone.

Finally, in common with many other Afro-

KING OLIVER'S JAZZ BAND in 1922. LOUIS ▶
ARMSTRONG is fourth from the left. The
pianist, LIL HARDING, was later to marry him.

American musicians, hip hop artists are fond of inventing grand names for themselves. The list includes GRAND-MASTER FLASH, GRANDMASTER MELLE MEL, THE WORLD CLASS WRECKING CRU, CAPTAIN ROCK, THE EGYPTIAN LOVER, KNIGHTS OF THE TURNTABLES and THE BAD BOYS.

Hip hop is in many ways very exclusive and deliberately seeks to confuse outsiders. At the same time, however, it has had an enormous influence on other forms of black music. In particular, it has given soul music the same kind of shot in the arm that punk gave to white rock music in the 'seventies.

JAZZ

Jazz is perhaps the most widely known and influential of all forms of Afro-American music. Like soul, the term jazz covers a vast array of musical styles, ranging from the traditional New Orleans sound of LOUIS ARMSTRONG to the free-form experiments of ORNETTE COLEMAN. All of these styles share certain key features, however, which have their roots in African music.

Rhythm
Although most jazz keeps to a basic two or four beats to the bar, the individual musicians play around with this time, anticipating or delaying notes, putting the

New Orleans jazz: a form of jazz which was born in the city of New Orleans and developed in Chicago during the 1920s. Also known as traditional jazz.

free-form jazz: a style of jazz developed during the 1960s in which the musicians make up the music as they go along.

emphasis in unexpected places and building up cross-rhythms.

As the great jazz musician DUKE ELLINGTON put it, "It don't mean a thing if it ain't got that swing." It is impossible to explain exactly what swing is. The singer, ELLA FITZGERALD, when asked for a definition of the term, came up with, "why, er – swing is – well, you sort of feel – uh, uh – I don't know – you just swing!" The bandleader, JIMMY LUNCEFORD, wrote a song which provides as good a definition as any:

"'Tain't watcha do, it's the way that you do it."

Instrumental tone

To a jazz musician an instrument is an extension of the voice, and it is possible to recognize the individual instrumental tone of a great jazz artist as easily as it is possible to recognize the voice of a singer.

Jazz musicians like to bend and slur notes, often sliding up to the first note of a phrase. Trumpet players use a variety of mutes to alter the tone of their instrument. Originally, many of these were home-made. The "plunger" mute, for example, was made from a rubber sink plunger. By squeezing the plunger to alter its shape, a musician could almost make the instrument talk. The greatest exponent of this style was BUBBER MILEY, who played in the Duke Ellington Orchestra. Other techniques include the use of vibrato,

vibrato: *a technique by which a singer or instrumentalist makes a note "wobble" slightly.*

flutter-tongueing, lip trills and partly depressed valves. Jazz musicians have also developed ways of hitting notes well beyond the accepted upper register of an instrument. In the 'seventies, the trumpeter, MILES DAVIS, started using electronic means to alter the tone of his instrument.

Improvisation

To improvise means to make something up as you go along. Improvisation is found in European as well as African music, but while it is a central feature of African music, in Europe it has often been regarded as a sort of musical showing-off. The importance of improvisation in jazz, therefore, is more likely to have come from African tradition.

There are three sorts of improvisation in jazz. In the first, the player just adds ornamentation to a tune, interpreting it in an original style. In the second, the basic chord pattern of a tune is used to provide a basis for something new. This is by far the most common form of improvisation. The tune is first played, in its original form, by the whole band. One musician takes the lead while the others weave counter-melodies. Each soloist in turn then steps forward to perform improvisations accompanied only by the rhythm section (usually piano, bass and drums). Each complete progression through the chords of the original tune is known as a "chorus". The number of choruses a soloist takes depends upon his or her inventiveness and stamina. Musicians talk about knowing the "changes" of a particular tune, by which they mean its chord

progression. The changes of some tunes are used again and again, the most popular being the "rhythm changes", so-called because they are the chords of GEORGE GERSHWIN'S "I've Got Rhythm".

A third sort of improvisation is "free form", pioneered by ORNETTE COLEMAN in the 1960s. There are no agreed chord changes and the musicians make the music up as they go along. The move towards free-form jazz prompted other musicians to look for alternatives to improvising around chord changes. The trumpeter MILES DAVIS and the saxophonist JOHN COLTRANE experimented with the use of *modes*. This was the system of scales used in medieval European music. Each mode started on a different note and had

JOHN COLTRANE in 1966. Coltrane was one of the dominant figures in jazz during the 'sixties. Tragically, he died of cancer in 1967.

flutter-tongueing: *a technique available to the players of brass instruments. A "drrr" sound is made with the tongue while sounding a note.*

lip trills: *A trill is the rapid alternation between one note and the one above or below it. It is possible to do this on a brass instrument by slightly altering the lip position.*

its own particular character. This can be heard by playing a series of scales on the piano using only the white notes. Indian music uses a similar system, where the modes are known as *ragas*. Davis said that the use of modes was "a challenge to see how melodically inventive you are. When you go this way, you can go on forever." Coltrane certainly met the challenge, producing improvised solos which went on for over fifteen minutes without ever becoming repetitive. Other musicians began to turn to non-European musical forms or to re-explore older Afro-American traditions such as the field holler.

Call-and-response

As we have seen, call-and-response is a vocal style used widely in African and Afro-American music. In jazz, it became an instrumental style which took several forms. Sometimes a line is played by a solo instrument and answered by the rest of the band. On other occasions a short phrase, or "riff", is played by one section of instruments and repeated by another. A third form of call-and-response is the "fours", or "chase choruses". Two musicians take alternate solos of four bars each, often trying to outdo each other. This is commonly used in the final chorus of a tune, with the soloists taking it in turns to trade fours with the drummer.

Music as a communal experience

Even in a concert hall, a jazz audience does not just sit still and listen. This would be regarded as very bad manners. On the contrary, the audience is expected to express its appreciation, applauding each soloist as he or she finishes and giving encouragement during particularly inventive passages. This follows African tradition, which sees music as a communal experience.

Another aspect of this sharing of music is the "jam session". A group of musicians comes together with no rehearsal to play just for the enjoyment of it. Jam sessions

The band-leader CAB CALLOWAY was a master of call-and-response style. Some jazz purists disliked his "Hi-de-hi-de-hi" vocal interludes, but he was a great influence on many later black entertainers. He was introduced to a whole new audience during the 'eighties through his role in the film The Blues Brothers.

can become very competitive, with each musician trying to play more inventive improvisations than the others. Traditionally, the jam session is where young musicians, or those with new ideas, have to prove their worth. They have to "put up or shut up". The birth of modern jazz can be traced to jam sessions which took place during the 1940s at a New York nightclub called Minton's Playhouse. It was here that young musicians such as the trumpet player DIZZY GILLESPIE and the brilliant alto saxophonist CHARLIE "YARD-BIRD" PARKER, developed the style known as be-bop. According to Gillespie, this is how it happened:

"Some of us began to jam at Minton's in Harlem in the early 'forties. But there were always some cats showing up there who couldn't blow at all but would take six or seven choruses to prove it. So, on afternoons before a session, [the pianist] Thelonious Monk and I began to work out some complex variations on chords and the like, and we used them at night to scare away the no-talent guys."
(Quoted in *Hear Me Talkin' To Ya* by Nat Shapiro and Nat Hentoff, Rinehart & Co. Inc., New York, 1955)

The development of jazz

It is possible to pinpoint seven major jazz styles which have developed since the 1920s:

1920s — New Orleans (or traditional jazz)
1930s — Big Bands (the "swing era")
1940s — Be-bop (the birth of modern jazz)
1950s — Cool jazz
        Hard bop
1960s — Free form
1970s — Jazz rock/jazz funk

None of these styles completely replaced what had gone before, however, and it is still possible to hear musicians playing any of them. Many musicians, such as Miles Davis, have been pioneers in more than one style.

The development of jazz was a complex affair, involving many social as well as musical issues. At some times, such as in the 1930s, jazz and popular music were one and the same thing, while in other periods, especially in the 'sixties, jazz

appealed only to a minority audience. It has often been claimed that jazz is dead, but those who make this claim are usually champions of one particular style of the music who believe that their favourite is the only "real" jazz.

There is not space here to go into these issues in the detail they deserve. The story of jazz needs a book to itself, but it can be summed up by two quotations, the first from the drummer JO JONES and the second from Charlie Parker.

"What is jazz? The closest thing I can get to saying what jazz is, is when you play what you feel. All jazz musicians express themselves through their instruments and they express the types of persons they are."

"Music is your own experience, your thoughts, your wisdom. If you don't live it, it won't come out of your horn."
(Both quoted in *Hear Me Talkin' To Ya*)

The role of women in jazz has been largely ignored. Two who did receive wide recognition, however, were the Kansas City pianist MARY LOU WILLIAMS (left) and the singer BILLIE HOLIDAY (above).

Mary Lou Williams was one of several famous pianists who emerged from Kansas City during the 'thirties. She was also well-known as an arranger. Billie Holiday was perhaps the greatest of all jazz singers. Despite the title of the film made about her life, Lady Sings The Blues, she rarely sang blues songs. Her gift was to take ordinary popular songs and deliver them with such feeling that they took on a new meaning. Like Bessie Smith, her personal life was a tragic one. "Lady Day", as she was known, died in 1959, aged only forty-four, a victim of alcohol and drug abuse.

PART FOUR

BLACK MUSIC IN SOUTH AMERICA

The music of South and Central America is a mixture of three traditions — American Indian, European and African. The Indian influence is strongest in Bolivia, Paraguay, Peru, Ecuador, Colombia, Venezuela and the inland areas of Brazil. The music of Argentina, Chile and Uruguay is the most European, while African traditions are most obvious along the coastal strip running from Brazil to Panama.

Having said this, it is not so easy to separate black and white musical styles in South America as it is in the U.S.A. There are two reasons for this. Firstly, the Spanish and Portuguese settlers in South America were not so anxious to keep the races separate as were those in North America. Secondly, as we have seen earlier, there were already links between African music and the music of Spain and Portugal before the slave trade started. In particular, the dramatic, rather nasal style of much Latin American music has its roots in the Muslim-influenced vocal techniques of both West Africa and Spain.

The Africanisms in Latin American music include the use of call-and-response and an emphasis on rhythm. The rhythm is more complex than that found in the black music of the U.S.A. and is characterized by a syncopated figure known as the *habanera*. The origins of this can be traced back to African drumming patterns. Drums and other percussion

The habanera is a rhythmic figure found throughout Latin America.

Although Britain, France and Holland had some ▶ *small colonies in South America, almost the whole of the continent was split between Spain and Portugal. The former Portuguese colonies form the vast country of Brazil, while most of the other countries in South America were once ruled by Spain. These former Spanish and Portuguese colonies are generally referred to as Latin America.*

instruments are very important and include bongoes, conga drums, timbales, claves, maracas and the *marimba*. Timbales are like small kettle-drums, each tuned to a different pitch. The name comes from the Arabic *at-tabl*, meaning a drum. Bongoes and the larger conga drums are also tuned. Claves are pieces of very hard wood which are tapped together. Maracas resemble the dried gourd rattles of West Africa, while the *marimba* is a descendant of the African xylophone. (In some parts of Latin America the African thumb piano mentioned earlier is known as the *marimbola*.)

The most "African" music in South America is that of the former Dutch colony of Surinam. Like Jamaica, this country had large settlements of runaway slaves, or *maroons*, who kept their African culture alive and won a large degree of independence. The best-known Latin American music, however, is that of Brazil.

The music of Brazil
The most obvious Africanism in Brazilian

conga: *a Latin American dance with three steps and a kick to each bar. Usually performed by dancers moving in single file.*

music is the strong link between music and dancing. The CONGA and the CONGADA have their roots in the Congo-Angola region from which the first Africans were taken to Brazil. The most widely known dance, however, is the SAMBA. It is related to African ring dances, with call-and-response singing led by a singer dancing

carnival: *The word comes from the Spanish, carne vale, meaning "goodbye to flesh". Carnivals traditionally take place just before the period of Lent, during which Christians give up eating meat. (In New Orleans, the carnival is known as Mardi Gras, which is French for "fat Tuesday".)*

45

A samba school in Rio.

in the centre of a circle of dancers and musicians. One of the main features of the annual carnival in Rio de Janeiro is the competition between the various samba "schools". These schools are societies of dancers and musicians made up of the people who live in the slums on the hills above Rio. Each one has a director who teaches and leads the dancing and singing. The sambas have the polyrhythmic drive which is a feature of African music. Percussion instruments provide the main musical backing. They are not always "real" instruments. As in Africa, almost anything can be used to make music – a knife tapped against a tin plate, a tin can, even a matchbox. In recent years, sambas have also borrowed ideas from other Afro-American sources, particularly jazz. The BOSSA NOVA was an attempt to mix samba and cool jazz.

There are also more "polite" versions of the samba, found in wealthier areas. These have a stronger European influence.

Another form of music in Brazil is CHORO. This takes the woodwind instruments of European military bands – flute, clarinet and saxophone – and adds a Latin American rhythm section. The music mixes European and Afro-American traditions in much the way that the first New Orleans jazz bands did, though the actual sound is very different.

---

military band: *also known as a "concert band". Unlike the brass band, military bands contain both brass and woodwind instruments.*

African influences elsewhere in South America

Outside Brazil, African influences can be heard in the music of the coastal regions of both Panama and Colombia.

The CUMBIA is a dance found in both those countries. It is possibly descended from an African dance called the *cumbe* and involves two dancers – a man and a woman. The woman dances in a circle around her partner and the accompanying musicians. The music is fiercely rhythmic, using drums and rattles. In the late 1970s, the jazz musician, CHARLES MINGUS, employed a Colombian percussion section to play with his band on the composition "Cumbia and Jazz Fusions". This mixed various forms of jazz with Colombian music and brought the latter to a wider audience. The rock musician, CARLOS SANTANA, also introduced Latin American rhythms to teenagers who might not otherwise have heard them.

South American musicians also had an influence on various forms of rhythm and blues and rock'n'roll, particularly in the southern United States. In Texas there is still a style of music known as TEX-MEX, which mixes rock music with elements of Latin American music. It tends to have only a local audience, but in the 'sixties SAM THE SHAM AND THE PHAROAHS had an international hit with a record called "Woolly Bully".

As with so many Afro-American styles, Latin American music has suffered from the fact that its more obviously African-influenced forms have been associated with the poorer sections of society. All too often, imitation of European fashions and culture has been seen as a sign of superior status. As a result, recorded examples of Latin American music have often been of a commercialized, "watered-down" variety. To many people, the term Latin American is still associated only with ballroom dancing. Although the music has never gained the same degree of recognition as black music from other parts of the Americas, its rhythms have had a great impact upon popular music. In particular, many of this century's dance crazes have originated in the dances of South America, which in turn have their roots in Africa.

PART FIVE

BLACK MUSIC IN THE CARIBBEAN

Each Caribbean island has its own musical traditions, depending upon which part of Africa its first black inhabitants came from, which European country (or countries) colonized it and the origin of later settlers. The music of three islands, however – CUBA, TRINIDAD and JAMAICA – has travelled further afield and has had a wider influence.

Cuba

Many of the general points made about Latin American music also apply to the music of Cuba. This island, the largest in the Caribbean, was a Spanish colony until the beginning of this century. When it gained independence, it was with

American help, but the United States then proceeded to influence Cuba as if it were an American colony instead. As in South America, African musical forms were confined to the poorer sections of society. In 1913, the government went so far as to ban the traditional carnival, while African religious cults had suffered persecution long before that. The Cuban Revolution of 1959 ended American domination of the island and the new government of Fidel Castro allied itself with African countries, such as Angola, which were also fighting for independence. Rather than being driven underground, the African elements in Cuban culture are now encouraged.

These African elements are most obvious in the RUMBA, a widely known Cuban dance whose influence has spread to other parts of Latin America and also

The Caribbean.

In 1959, CASTRO and his revolutionary army entered the capital, Havana.

back to parts of West Africa (see Part Six). In its original form, the dance was performed by a couple surrounded by a circle of singers and musicians. The singing used a call-and-response form, while the musical backing relied upon percussion instruments. A steady beat was provided by the claves, and complex rhythms could be built around it. A more westernized form of the rumba became very popular during the 1930s, not only in Cuba but also in the U.S.A.

The MAMBO developed from the rumba,

adding guitars, saxophones and trumpets to the line-up of instruments. The word mambo possibly comes from the Bantu word, *mambe*, meaning "a song". During the 'twenties, the increasing influence of the United States led to a craze for jazz in Cuba. By the 'thirties, however, Cuban musicians were integrating elements of jazz with mambo, rather than merely copying the American music. This development worked both ways and be-bop musicians such as Dizzy Gillespie and Charlie Parker recorded with the Cuban bandleader, MACHITO, during the 'fifties, producing a style which was labelled CU-BOP. Later jazz musicians, the saxophonist ARCHIE SHEPP for example, have also called on the services of Cuban percussionists.

Cuban musicians at carnival time.

Trinidad . . .

The music of Trinidad is strongly influenced by that of Latin America. The island is a melting pot of different cultures – African, Spanish, French, British, East Indian and Chinese. These elements are found in most Trinidadian music, but the African influence is strongest in the country's two best-known musical forms, CALYPSO and STEEL BAND.

. . . Calypso

The tradition of the African griots – singing songs about events in the news and important or famous people – is found throughout the Caribbean. In Jamaica it is known as MENTO. Puerto Ricans living in New York developed the style known as SALSA which has spread to other parts of Latin America.

In Trinidad, a form known as *kaiso* emerged about a hundred years ago. Even today, the word kaiso is used in Trinidad as well as the more modern name, CALYPSO. The roots of the music go back even further, to satirical songs sung in French Creole in the eighteenth century.

The rhythms of calypso owe much to Latin American music, with a particular emphasis on percussion. The traditional instruments for accompanying the songs were scrapers, rattles, drums, bottles and knives. Later on, more sophisticated instrumentation and arrangements were developed, borrowing ideas from Cuban music and jazz. Calypsonians have always regarded themselves as larger-than-life characters and have adopted suitable titles – EDWARD THE CONFESSOR, ATTILA THE HUN, THE ROARING LION, THE MIGHTY SPARROW and so on. As well as being about topical events, calypsoes are often very frank about sex. In 1930, the authorities in Trinidad tried to ban calypso, using anti-obscenity laws as an excuse. The calypsonian Attila made the following response:

"To say these songs are sacrilegious,
obscene or profane

A calypso singer.

Is only a lie and a dirty shame.
If the calypso is indecent then I must
insist
So is Shakespeare's Venus and
Adonis."

Just as the samba schools are an important part of the carnival in Rio, so the calypso "tents" are a feature of the Trinidad carnival. The "tents" are the headquarters of the various carnival bands. The different singers compete to find the "King of the Calypsonians". A feature of the tent competitions is the war of words, or PICCONG, in which singers take it in turn to insult each other in their songs. During the 'thirties and 'forties, this became a contest to see who could use the most complicated language. The masters of this style were Attila the Hun and The Roaring Lion.

From the 1970s onwards, the influence of soul and reggae upon calypso became more pronounced. The result was a new

51

rhythm, known as SOCA (soul + calypso), with songs in which the topical content was less important. Television and newspapers have taken over the calypsonian's role as a teller of news to a certain extent, but many calypsoes still comment on more general issues. This is apparent in the songs of younger calypsonians such as DAVID RUDDER.

...Steel band

Steel drums, or pans, are made from large

Making a steel drum.

oil drums. Part of the drum is cut off, leaving up to half a metre for the body. A series of dents, each of which gives a different note when struck, is made on the top surface by heating and hammering. This is a highly skilled job, to which David Rudder pays tribute in his song "The Hammer". There are several different sizes of pan, ranging from the "ping pong", which can play many notes, to the bass, or "boom", which can produce only a few. The shorter the pan is cut, the higher the notes it produces and the more of them.

Steel bands are the latest in a long line of drum orchestras which have been a feature of the Trinidad carnival. The authorities frowned on these, banning them altogether in 1883. The following years saw battles breaking out as the police tried to enforce this ban. One way around the law was to use bamboo sticks instead of drums. Different lengths of bamboo produced different notes when banged on the floor or beaten together. The resulting music was known as TAMBOO BAMBOO. Other instruments included bottles tapped with spoons, but during the 1930s, these were replaced by dustbin lids and biscuit tins. As musicians experimented with these instruments, gradually learning how to tune them to definite pitches, they replaced the bamboo sticks altogether. During the 1940s, the fifty-five-gallon oil drum was found to be the perfect raw material for making steel drums.

Steel bands met stiff opposition from the authorities and there were attempts to ban them altogether. The opposition stemmed both from those who objected to the noise and from those who thought that steel bands were unmusical and low-class. There were still many wealthier people in the Caribbean who thought that copying European culture was a sign of status. During the 'forties, members of steel bands were arrested and given heavy fines. In the end, the matter was taken up by a government committee and in 1950 a steel band association was formed. The success of the TRINIDAD ALL STARS PERCUSSION ORCHESTRA at the 1951 Festival of Britain helped to make the future of the music secure. Those who still thought European culture was the best were satisfied by the fact that the orchestra's repertoire included extracts from Tchaikovsky's First Piano Concerto. Indeed, a feature of steel bands has always been their enthusiasm for tackling almost any form of music.

From being almost illegal, steel bands have gone on to become one of the Caribbean's best-known musical forms. In 1954, a member of the Trinidadian legislative, speaking in favour of banning steel bands, said that he would like to see talented musicians given encouragement to "express themselves musically". Ironically, it is the very steel bands which he sought to abolish which have provided this vehicle for musical expression.

Jamaica...

Jamaican folk music is a mixture of African and British traditions. The fife and drum bands found in rural areas, for example, are an Afro-American version of the British military bands of the eighteenth century. The island is best-known, though, for a form of music which has emerged only over the last thirty years – REGGAE.

...Reggae

During the 1950s, many young people in Jamaica were becoming bored with the folk music of the island and with *mento*, the Jamaican form of calypso. Looking for something they could call their own, they turned to the music that had been introduced to the island by black American servicemen stationed there during the war – rhythm and blues. The New Orleans style of FATS DOMINO and FRANKIE FORD was particularly popular. New Orleans, with its French and Spanish connections, had always been almost part of the Caribbean. Its rhythm and blues style had several Latin American elements and a heavy off-beat not unlike the Jamaican mento rhythm. The demand for the music was enormous and disc-jockeys took their sound systems around the island, playing for what became known as "blues parties". They developed loyal followings and gave themselves grand names, just like the calypsonians. Each tried to find records not possessed by rival systems, scratching the labels off records to keep their origin secret. It wasn't long before some had the idea of making their own recordings, using local talent, rather than importing records from the United States.

The result, recorded in makeshift studios in Kingston, was a mixture of rhythm and blues and mento. It became known as BLUE BEAT or SKA. In its early years, the music had a lot in common with calypso. Many of the songs were about events in the news, especially the problems faced by the "rude boys", teenage dropouts from Jamaican society. There were also cover versions of rhythm and blues hits and other popular songs. The SKATALITES' "Independent Anniversary Ska", for example, is an instrumental version of The Beatles' "I Should Have Known Better".

The music was generally up-tempo, with the bass and drums emphasizing the first and third beats of the bar while the other instruments played four strong off-beats. Bands included a front line of trumpet, trombone and saxes, many of the musicians having a jazz background.

During the 'sixties there was a change of

Festival of Britain: *a large-scale festival held on the South Bank of the River Thames in 1951. The aim was to cheer people up in the years following the Second World War.*

---

off-beat: *an emphasis on the second half of a beat or on the second and fourth beats in four/four time.*

style. ROCKSTEADY, as it became known, was much slower. The bass and drums continued to emphasize the first and third beats of the bar but the other instruments dropped the four off-beats in favour of a stress on the second and fourth beats of the bar. The trumpets and saxes played a less dominant role, their place being taken by guitar and piano. Vocalists began to look to soul singers such as OTIS REDDING for inspiration. There are two explanations put forward for this change. One is that a spell of particularly hot and dry weather made dancers want something slower. Another looks towards the increasing influence of the Rastafarians and their music.

The RASTAFARIANS worship the late emperor Haile Selassie of Ethiopia. He was also known as Ras Tafari and his official titles included King of Kings and The Conquering Lion of Judah. He belonged to a royal family which claimed descent from King David. Rastas believe that they are exiled from their roots in Africa, just as the Israelites were exiled in Babylon. For them, Zion is not Jerusalem but Ethiopia. Their music mixes the drumming of the neo-African cults discussed in Part Two, with the hymns of the Revival churches. Although the Rastafarian religion developed in the 'thirties, it did not become widespread until the 'sixties, when Haile Selassie visited Jamaica. Rastafarianism seemed to offer hope to the unemployed and poor people of Kingston's shanty towns. The influence of the Rastas became more obvious in Jamaican popular music, not only in the way it sounded but also in its

---

Revival churches: *During the nineteenth century, there was a religious movement in America, known as The Great Revival. This spread to the Caribbean and the Revival churches stem from that time. They place great emphasis upon the receiving of personal messages from God and their services involve much singing and chanting.*

---

lyrics. It became a powerful vehicle for expressing both hope and anger.

Reggae developed out of rocksteady in the late 'sixties. (In 1968, TOOTS AND THE MAYTALS had a hit with "Do The Reggay", the first record to use this new name.) In the following years, the "dub" style of production was introduced by LEE "SCRATCH" PERRY. He would take the various tracks made in a recording session and re-mix them to produce something of his own. The emphasis was on the rhythm, with only fragmented snatches of melody being used. At the same time, "toasting" was developed. This consists of a disc jockey, or "mike chanter", talking over a pre-recorded rhythm track. The words are largely improvised and include a mixture of religious and political messages and nonsense rhymes. There is also a fair amount of boasting and often artists will engage in a war of words in the way that calypsonians do.

As a result of these developments, rhythm became more important than melody in reggae, with the interplay between drums and bass being the dominant feature. Two of the best-known reggae musicians are the drummer SLY DUNBAR and the bass player ROBBIE SHAKESPEARE. Not only are they in demand in Jamaica, but they have also been employed as backing musicians by artists as different as GRACE JONES and IAN DURY. Just as jazz musicians will use the chord changes of one tune to improvise new ones, so reggae musicians will use the rhythm pattern.

The music has developed in several directions since the early seventies, ranging from heavy, Rasta-influenced dub to the softer, romantic "lovers' rock". Some artists have also found success with a much wider audience, the most notable of these being BOB MARLEY. Marley came to the notice of rock fans in 1973 when Island Records gave the album "Catch A Fire" the kind of packaging and promotion previously given only to rock albums. In fact, his recording career started twelve

BOB MARLEY, 1974.

moved to the United States to live with his mother. Faced with being drafted to fight in Vietnam, he returned to Jamaica. The Wailers reformed, adding bass player ASTON BARRETT and his brother CARLTON BARRETT on drums. After some success with producer Lee Perry, they were signed up by Island Records.

After two albums, Tosh and Livingstone left the group and it became known as Bob Marley and The Wailers. The first album released under this new name was "Natty Dread". The music had a strong gospel influence, emphasized by the addition of a female vocal trio, THE I-THREES. The lyrics dealt with Rastafarianism and the need for political change, but there were also love songs such as "No Woman No Cry", his first British hit single. Marley rapidly became a superstar, in demand through-out the world. Unlike so many other superstars, Marley did not forget his roots nor change his beliefs. His political views led to an assassination attempt which he answered by calling the leaders of Jamaica's two feuding political parties to attend his "One Love Peace Concert". At the end of the concert, he called them to the stage and made them join hands above his head. As one admirer put it, he looked like Jesus between the two thieves.

He was also passionately concerned with the independence struggle in Zimbabwe. In 1978, he was awarded the Third World Peace Medal at the United Nations and in the following year, The Wailers were invited to play . at the Zimbabwe Independence celebrations. At the height of his popularity and influence, Marley died of cancer on 11th May, 1981. A month previously, he had been awarded Jamaica's Order Of Merit, and on his death, he was given a full state funeral.

years earlier in 1961. After a few unsuccessful solo efforts, he teamed up with Peter McIntosh (PETER TOSH) and Bunny Livingstone (BUNNY WAILER) to form THE WAILING WAILERS. At first, the Wailers were a vocal group, backed by ska musicians such as The Skatalites. They had several hits in Jamaica but made no money (at that time, Jamaican record company owners were notorious for exploiting their artists) and in 1966, Marley

PART SIX

MODERN AFRICAN MUSIC

Part One dealt with the main features of traditional African music. Since the late 1950s, Afro-American styles have been finding their way back to Africa where they have been "re-Africanized". This modern African music varies from country to country and the following is an outline of some of the major forms it takes.

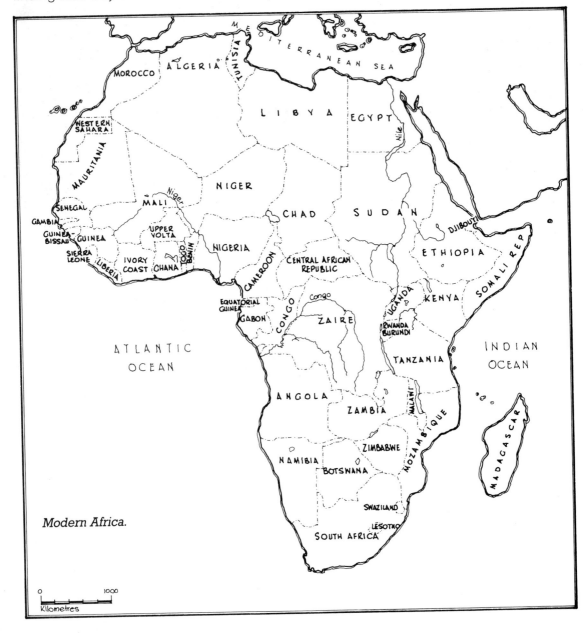

Modern Africa.

One of the younger Nigerian ju-ju musicians, SEGUN ADEWALE.

Nigeria/Ghana

HIGHLIFE was the first modern African urban style to emerge. It sounds very similar to calypso, but there is some debate as to whether calypso influenced highlife or whether both stem from a similar West African tradition. In the 1960s, highlife was the most popular form of music in West Africa, but its influence is now confined to Ghana and Eastern Nigeria.

It has been replaced in other areas by JU-JU. This has its roots in traditional Yoruba music, particularly in its use of talking drums. These engage in call-and-response dialogue with the singers. During the 'fifties, electric guitars were introduced and became a vital part of the music. They are used in a very different manner to that employed by rock musicians, however. A band might contain six guitarists, weaving patterns together rather than taking individual solos. Ju-ju musicians also like to exploit the "singing" qualities of the guitar, and the use of Hawaiian or steel guitars, normally associated with country and western music, is common. Many bands also use synthesizers and have begun to explore the dub techniques of reggae. The best-known ju-ju musician is KING SUNNY ADE, who has recently been given the kind of promotion by Island Records that they gave to Bob Marley.

Hawaiian guitar: *a fretless guitar which is placed horizontally. Instead of plucking the strings, the player slides a metal bar along them. The steel guitar is an electrically amplified version of the same instrument.*

57

The nearest to a Nigerian superstar in the Marley mould, though, is FELA ANIKULAPO KUTI. Fela calls his music AFRO-BEAT and it has a very strong jazz influence. It is the political message of the music which is more important, however. Fela Kuti pours scorn upon the multi-national companies and the African leaders he feels have "sold out" to them. His outspoken attacks have led to periods in prison but he insists that eventually he will be made president by the people. His stage show deliberately sets out to emphasize African traditions which Europeans tried to downgrade and involves drama and dancing as well as music. He makes much use of what was referred to in Part One (page 7) as "creative repetition", and engages in long

---

multi-national companies: *large companies operating in several countries.*

FAN FAN, an exponent of the Congolese guitar style. He plays with the London-based group, SOMO SOMO.

call-and-response sessions with his backing singers.

Zaire (formerly the Belgian Congo)

Although the music of Ghana and Nigeria was the first to reach a wider audience, it is now being threatened, so far as popularity goes, by SOUKOUS, which comes from Zaire. Modern Congolese music has its origins in the rumba, but the brass lines of the Cuban music are played instead by guitarists. Congolese guitar style, like that of ju-ju, relies upon the interplay between several musicians rather than solo efforts. Its greatest stars are the musicians FRANCO and TABU LEY. The influence of the music has spread beyond Zaire to Kenya, Tanzania and Uganda. Many of the best-known East African bands, such as Tanzania's ORCHESTRE MAKASSY, come orginally from Zaire.

Southern Africa

In this area of Africa, music has become closely linked with political struggles. In

Zimbabwe, CHIMURENGA music was created during the struggle for independence. The authorities banned political songs, but musicians got around this by concealing political messages in songs which were, on the surface, about

The power of music. Black and white fans at a Johannesburg concert in 1986 give the Black Power salute.

something else. The best-known of these chimurenga musicians is THOMAS

MAPFUMO, whose music shows an increasing reggae influence.

Many of South Africa's best musicians are living in exile because of their opposition to the system of apartheid which separates people according to their racial origins and leaves all power with the white minority. The South African government, recognizing the power of music, has banned many artists. For instance, anyone caught listening to records by MIRIAM MAKEBA risks imprisonment. Other artists who prefer (or are forced) to live outside South Africa include DOLLAR BRAND and HUGH MASEKELA. These are both jazz musicians, but there is also a strong tradition within South Africa of black township music. This is generally grouped together under the title MBAQANGA. Most of the musicians hold down other jobs and can face difficulties getting their music recorded. The music has a very different sound from that of other parts of Africa. Its rhythm has certain similarities to reggae, though without the strong off-beat. The bass guitar plays a very important role, as does the piano accordion.

Black South African music does not have the variety of instruments found elsewhere in the continent, largely because the raw materials to make them are in short supply. As a result, the polyrhythms supplied elsewhere by instruments are provided instead by the human voice. A steady rhythm is set up with handclaps, drums or rattles around which the voices weave complex patterns. Unaccompanied group vocal music, known as MBUBE, is common throughout South Africa. Spontaneous singing of this kind is also a feature of political gatherings.

Other modern African styles

MBALAX is the name given to a form of music found in Senegal. Despite making use of modern studio techniques, Senegalese musicians still favour the use of the *kora*, a twenty-one-string harp, which is one of the country's traditional instruments.

MAKOSSA is a rhythm found in Cameroun. In the early 'seventies, MANU DIBANGO had an international disco hit with "Soul Makossa" and he has since experimented at mixing makossa with other styles, including electro.

*　　*　　*

This "re-Africanization" of Afro-American music takes our story full circle. Many of the forms of music discussed in the previous chapters developed independently of each other, but modern communications mean that fusions of different styles are becoming more and more common. The process which started with the transportation of millions of Africans to the Americas in the sixteenth, seventeenth and eighteenth centuries is by no means over.

DATE LIST

698 – Muslim conquests in North Africa
711 – Muslim conquests in Spain
900 – West African empire of Ghana at its height
1325 – West African empire of Mali at its height
1433 – Portuguese begin their exploration of West African coast
1492 – Moors expelled from Spain
Columbus reaches West Indies
1493 – West African Songhai Empire at its height, Timbuktu a great centre of learning
1532 – Portuguese take Africans to Brazil as slaves
1562 – Hawkins becomes first English slave trader
1606 – Dutch enter slave trade
1776 – American Declaration of Independence
1792 – Denmark first European country to abolish slave trade
1807 – Britain abolishes slave trade
1838 – Slavery abolished in British colonies
1848 – Slavery abolished in French colonies
1861 – American Civil War
1863 – Slavery abolished in the United States
1873 – Ashanti War – Britain annexes Ashanti Kingdom in West Africa
1879 – Zulu War in South Africa
1886 – Abolition of slavery in Spanish colonies

1914-18 – First World War
1929 – Wall Street Crash – start of the Depression
1939-45 – Second World War
1951 – Mau Mau revolt in Kenya
1958 – Ghana gains independence, followed by other British and French colonies in Africa
1959 – Cuban Revolution
1960 – Sharpeville Massacre – Police open fire on black strikers in South Africa
1962 – Jamaica and Trinidad and Tobago gain independence
1963 – Start of Civil Rights Movement in U.S.A.
Assassination of John F. Kennedy
1965 – Demonstrations in U.S.A. and Britain against the Vietnam War
Assassination of Malcolm X
1967 – Riots in several American cities
1968 – Assassination of Martin Luther King
1970 – End of Civil War in Nigeria
1974 – Revolution in Ethiopia – Haile Selassie deposed
1975 – Angola wins independence after 500 years of Portuguese rule
Last American soldiers leave Vietnam
1979 – End of white minority rule in Zimbabwe (Rhodesia)
1986 – State of Emergency in South Africa

DISCOGRAPHY

Some forms of music are much harder to find on record than others. The following list gives an idea of what is currently available. (Thanks to Martin Salisbury of the Record Trade Centre in Beckenham for his assistance.)

Traditional African music

AFRICAN JOURNEY: VOLUMES 1 & 2 – Sonet – SNTF 666/667
AFRICAN RHYTHMS AND INSTRUMENTS: VOLUMES 1, 2, & 3 – Lyrichord – LLST 7328/38/39

Neo-African music

FROM SLAVERY TO FREEDOM – Music from Surinam – Lyrichord – LLST 7354
PRISON WORK SONGS – Arhoolie (import) – 2012
CARIBBEAN SONGS AND DANCES – Nonesuch Explorer – H 72047
AFRO-BRAZILIAN RELIGIOUS SONGS – Lyrichord – LLST 7315

Gospel

THE SOUL OF BLACK MUSIC: VOLUMES 1 & 2 – Sonet SNTF 795/6

Blues

STORY OF THE BLUES – CBS – 22135
  (An excellent two-album anthology covering most aspects of the development of the blues)
STORY OF THE BLUES VOLUMES 1 & 2 – CBS – 66426
  (A four-album version of the above with extra tracks)
BEST OF THE CHICAGO BLUES – Vanguard – VSD 1
THE BEST OF B.B. KING – Chiswick – CH 30
ZYDECO – Arhoolie (import) – 1009

Soul

RAY CHARLES – "I CAN'T STOP LOVING YOU" – Pickwick – SSP 3075
THE BEST OF JAMES BROWN – Polydor – 2391 529
ATLANTIC HISTORY – Atlantic – A 00484
16 BIG HITS – Motown – STMF 7001
  (Actually 32 hits, 16 each from the early and late 'sixties)
PHILADELPHIA CLASSICS – Philadelphia International – PIR 88274
PARLIAMENT – "GLORYHALLASTOOPID" – Casablanca – NBLP 7195
TROUBLE FUNK – "DROP THE BOMB" – Sugarhill – SHLP 1006
CRUCIAL ELECTRO – Streetsounds – ELCST 999
  (The Streetsounds series of compilations is an excellent source of contemporary black dance music)

Jazz

THE LOUIS ARMSTRONG LEGEND – EMI – SH 404
DUKE ELLINGTON "GREATEST HITS" – CBS – 21059
COUNT BASIE – "SWINGING THE BLUES" – Affinity – AFS 1010
CHARLIE PARKER/DIZZY GILLESPIE – EMI – 2M 056 64847
MILES DAVIS – "BIRTH OF THE COOL" – Capitol (cassette) – TC CAPS 1024
ART BLAKEY QUINTET – "A NIGHT AT BIRDLAND" – Blue Note – BST 81521
ORNETTE COLEMAN – "FREE JAZZ" – Atlantic – ATL 50240
JOHN COLTRANE – "THE ART OF JOHN COLTRANE" – Atlantic – K 60052
MILES DAVIS – "BITCHES BREW" – CBS – 66236
THE BEST OF BLUE NOTE: VOLUMES 1 & 2 – Blue Note – BST2 84429/33

South America

AMAZONIA – CULT MUSIC OF NORTHERN BRAZIL – Lyrichord – LLST 7300
BLACK MUSIC OF BAHAI (BRAZIL) – Albatross (Italy) – VPA 8318
  (Distributed by Triple Earth, tel. 01-995 7059)

ORFEU NEGRO (BLACK ORPHEUS) – Philips (France) – 8124 731
BRAZIL TODAY – Polydor – 8128 491
JOAO GILBERTO – "BRASIL" – Mercury – 6328 382
GILBERTO GIL – "NIGHTINGALE" – Elektra – K 52120
CHARLES MINGUS – "CUMBIA AND JAZZ FUSION" – Atlantic – K 50486

Caribbean
CELIA CRUZ – "CELIA AND WILLIE" – Salsa (import) – JMUS 93
MACHITO & HIS AFRO-CUBAN SALSEROS – Pablo – 2625 712
EARLY AFRO-CUBAN SONGS – Albatross – VPA 8445
THE TRINIDAD STEEL BAND – Nonesuch Explorer – H 72016
THE DESPERADOES – Charisma – CLASS 11
MIGHTY SPARROW – "PEACE AND LOVE" – Trojan – TRLS 159
THIS IS SOCA – Oval – OVLP 512
THIS IS SOCA 2 – London – LONLP 20
SOCA TRAIN – London – LONLP 2
BYRON LEE & THE DRAGONAIRES – "THIS IS CARNIVAL" – Dynamic – DYLP 3006
INTENSIFIED – ORIGINAL SKA – Island – IRSP 12
CREATION ROCKERS – Trojan – TRLS 180 – TRLS 185
   (A six-album history of reggae)
REGGAE GREATS – THE D.J.s – Island – IRG 4
BOB MARLEY – "EXODUS" – Island – ILPS 9498

Modern African music
AFRICAN MUSIC (Highlife) – Vertigo – 8144 801
KING SUNNY ADE – "SYNCHRO SYSTEM" – Island – ILPS 9737
FELA KUTI – "BLACK PRESIDENT" – Arista – SPART 1167
SOUND D'AFRIQUE – Island – ISSP 4003
   (An anthology of Congolese-style music)
MANU D'BANGO – "SOUL MAKOSSA" – Discovery Records – SCO 9037
M'BILIA BEL – "BOYA YE" – Sterns 1012
ORCHESTRE MAKASSY – "AGWAYA" – Virgin – V2236
VIVA ZIMBABWE – Rough Trade – ELP 2001
HUGH MASEKELA – "TECHNO BUSH" – Jive Afrika – HIP 11
DOLLAR BRAND (ABDULLAH IBRAHIM) – "EKAYA" – Ekpa – 005
MIRIAM MAKEBA – "THE VOICE OF AFRICA" – RCA – 2621228
SOWETO COMPILATION – Rough Trade – Rough 37
   (An anthology of black township music)

Records of Latin American (including Caribbean) music can be obtained from "TUMI"
Latin American craft centres at 2, New Bond Street Place, Bath, Avon BA1 1BL (tel. 0225
62367/64736) and 22, Chalk Farm Road, Camden Town, London NW1 (tel. 01 485 4152)

INDEX